Windows 7 Shortcut Keys

By

U. C-Abel Books.

COPYRIGHT

All Rights Reserved

First Edition: 2015

Table of Contents

INTRODUCTION

This book, Windows 7 Shortcut Keys, is like salvation sent into computing world to help windows 7 users to do greater than they have been doing.

It is awesomely organized in a tabular form with its *Shortcut Keys* and *Actions* neatly separated.

Use your computer to the amazement of others; attract appreciation from your boss, colleagues, neighbours, friends and well-wishers through the use of windows 7 shortcut keys listed in this book

---

ACKNOWLEDGEMENT

U. C-Abel Books will not take all the credits for the shortcuts listed in this book, but will share them with Microsoft Corporation because most of the shortcuts came from them and "are used with permission from Microsoft".

WINDOWS 7 KEYBOARD SHORTCUTS

a.) EASE OF ACCESS KEYBOARD SHORTCUTS

The table below contains keyboard shortcuts that can make your computer easier to use.

Note: "Shortcut" here means the key combination used to achieve the **"Action"** which is the result of the shortcut (key combination) used.

Shortcut	Action
Right Shift for eight seconds	Turn Filter Keys on and off
Left Alt+Left Shift+PrtScn (or PrtScn)	Turn High Contrast on or off
Left Alt+Left Shift+Num Lock	Turn Mouse Keys on or off
Shift five times	Turn Sticky Keys on or off
Num Lock for five seconds	Turn Toggle Keys on or off
Windows logo key ⊞ +U	Open the Ease of Access Center

b.) GENERAL KEYBOARD SHORTCUTS

The table below contains general keyboard shortcuts.

Shortcut	Action
F1	Display Help
Ctrl+C (or Ctrl+Insert)	Copy the selected item
Ctrl+X	Cut the selected item
Ctrl+V (or Shift+Insert)	Paste the selected item
Ctrl+Z	Undo an action
Ctrl+Y	Redo an action
Delete (or Ctrl+D)	Delete the selected item and move it to the Recycle Bin
Shift+Delete	Delete the selected item without moving it to the Recycle Bin first
F2	Rename the selected item
Ctrl+Right Arrow	Move the cursor to the beginning of the next word
Ctrl+Left Arrow	Move the cursor to the beginning of the previous word
Ctrl+Down Arrow	Move the cursor to the beginning of the next paragraph
Ctrl+Up Arrow	Move the cursor to the beginning of the previous paragraph
Ctrl+Shift with an arrow key	Select a block of text
Shift with any arrow key	Select more than one item in a window or on the desktop, or select text within a document

Ctrl with any arrow key+Spacebar	Select multiple individual items in a window or on the desktop
Ctrl+A	Select all items in a document or window
F3	Search for a file or folder
Alt+Enter	Display properties for the selected item
Alt+F4	Close the active item, or exit the active program
Alt+Spacebar	Open the shortcut menu for the active window
Ctrl+F4	Close the active document (in programs that allow you to have multiple documents open simultaneously)
Alt+Tab	Switch between open items
Ctrl+Alt+Tab	Use the arrow keys to switch between open items
Ctrl+Mouse scroll wheel	Change the size of icons on the desktop
Windows logo key ⊞+Tab	Cycle through programs on the taskbar by using Aero Flip 3-D
Ctrl+Windows logo key ⊞+Tab	Use the arrow keys to cycle through programs on the taskbar by using Aero Flip 3-D
Alt+Esc	Cycle through items in the order in which they were opened
F6	Cycle through screen elements in a window or on the desktop

F4	Display the address bar list in Windows Explorer
Shift+F10	Display the shortcut menu for the selected item
Ctrl+Esc	Open the Start menu
Alt+underlined letter	Display the corresponding menu
Alt+underlined letter	Perform the menu command (or other underlined command)
F10	Activate the menu bar in the active program
Right Arrow	Open the next menu to the right, or open a submenu
Left Arrow	Open the next menu to the left, or close a submenu
F5 (or Ctrl+R)	Refresh the active window
Alt+Up Arrow	View the folder one level up in Windows Explorer
Esc	Cancel the current task
Ctrl+Shift+Esc	Open Task Manager
Shift when you insert a CD	Prevent the CD from automatically playing
Left Alt+Shift	Switch the input language when multiple input languages are enabled
Ctrl+Shift	Switch the keyboard layout when multiple keyboard layouts are enabled
Right or Left Ctrl+Shift	Change the reading direction of text in right-to-left reading languages

c.) DIALOG BOX

A small window that communicates information to the user and prompts them for a response.

Dialog box keyboard shortcuts

The table below contains keyboard shortcuts for use in dialog boxes.

Shortcut	Action
Ctrl+Tab	Move forward through tabs
Ctrl+Shift+Tab	Move back through tabs
Tab	Move forward through options
Shift+Tab	Move back through options
Alt+underlined letter	Perform the command (or select the option) that goes with that letter
Enter	Replaces clicking the mouse for many selected commands
Spacebar	Select or clear the check box if the active option is a check box
Arrow keys	Select a button if the active option is a group of option buttons
F1	Display Help
F4	Display the items in the active list
Backspace	Open a folder one level up if a folder is selected in the Save As or Open dialog box

d.) WINDOWS LOGO KEY

A key on Microsoft Computer keyboard with its logo. Search for this ⊞ on your keyboard.

Windows logo key keyboard shortcuts
The table below contains keyboard shortcuts that use the Windows logo key ⊞.

Shortcut	Action
Windows logo key ⊞	Open or close the Start menu.
Windows logo key ⊞ +Pause	Display the System Properties dialog box.
Windows logo key ⊞ +D	Display the desktop.
Windows logo key ⊞ +M	Minimize all windows.
Windows logo key ⊞ +Shift+M	Restore minimized windows to the desktop.
Windows logo key ⊞ +E	Open Computer.
Windows logo key ⊞ +F	Search for a file or folder.
Ctrl+Windows logo key ⊞+F	Search for computers (if you're on a network).
Windows logo key ⊞ +L	Lock your computer or switch users.
Windows logo key ⊞ +R	Open the Run dialog box.
Windows logo key ⊞ +T	Cycle through programs on the taskbar.

Windows logo key ⊞ +number	Start the program pinned to the taskbar in the position indicated by the number. If the program is already running, switch to that program.
Shift+Windows logo key ⊞+number	Start a new instance of the program pinned to the taskbar in the position indicated by the number.
Ctrl+Windows logo key ⊞+number	Switch to the last active window of the program pinned to the taskbar in the position indicated by the number.
Alt+Windows logo key ⊞+number	Open the Jump List for the program pinned to the taskbar in the position indicated by the number.
Windows logo key ⊞ +Tab	Cycle through programs on the taskbar by using Aero Flip 3-D.
Ctrl+Windows logo key ⊞+Tab	Use the arrow keys to cycle through programs on the taskbar by using Aero Flip 3-D.
Ctrl+Windows logo key ⊞+B	Switch to the program that displayed a message in the notification area.
Windows logo key ⊞ +Spacebar	Preview the desktop.

Windows logo key ⊞ +Up Arrow	Maximize the window.
Windows logo key ⊞ +Left Arrow	Maximize the window to the left side of the screen.
Windows logo key ⊞ +Right Arrow	Maximize the window to the right side of the screen.
Windows logo key ⊞ +Down Arrow	Minimize the window.
Windows logo key ⊞ +Home	Minimize all but the active window.
Windows logo key ⊞ +Shift+Up Arrow	Stretch the window to the top and bottom of the screen.
Windows logo key ⊞ +Shift+Left Arrow or Right Arrow	Move a window from one monitor to another.
Windows logo key ⊞ +P	Choose a presentation display mode.
Windows logo key ⊞ +G	Cycle through gadgets.
Windows logo key ⊞ +U	Open Ease of Access Center.
Windows logo key ⊞ +X	Open Windows Mobility Center.

e.) WINDOWS EXPLORER

Windows Explorer is the file management application in Windows. *Windows Explorer* can be used to navigate your hard drive and display the contents of the folders and subfolders you use to organize your files on your hard drive.

Windows Explorer keyboard shortcuts

The following table contains keyboard shortcuts for working with Windows Explorer windows or folders.

Shortcut	Action
Ctrl+N	Open a new window
Ctrl+W	Close the current window
Ctrl+Shift+N	Create a new folder
End	Display the bottom of the active window
Home	Display the top of the active window
F11	Maximize or minimize the active window
Ctrl+Period (.)	Rotate a picture clockwise
Ctrl+Comma (,)	Rotate a picture counter-clockwise
Num Lock+Asterisk (*) on numeric keypad	Display all subfolders under the selected folder
Num Lock+Plus Sign (+) on numeric keypad	Display the contents of the selected folder

Num Lock+Minus Sign (-) on numeric keypad	Collapse the selected folder
Left Arrow	Collapse the current selection (if it's expanded), or select the parent folder
Alt+Enter	Open the Properties dialog box for the selected item
Alt+P	Display the preview pane
Alt+Left Arrow	View the previous folder
Backspace	View the previous folder
Right Arrow	Display the current selection (if it's collapsed), or select the first subfolder
Alt+Right Arrow	View the next folder
Alt+Up Arrow	View the parent folder
Ctrl+Shift+E	Display all folders above the selected folder
Ctrl+Mouse scroll wheel	Change the size and appearance of file and folder icons
Alt+D	Select the address bar
Ctrl+E	Select the search box
Ctrl+F	Select the search box

f.) TASKBAR

The *taskbar* is the long horizontal bar at the bottom of your computer screen.

Taskbar keyboard shortcuts

The table below contains keyboard shortcuts for working with items on the taskbar.

Shortcut	Action
Shift+Click on a taskbar button	Open a program or quickly open another instance of a program
Ctrl+Shift+Click on a taskbar button	Open a program as an administrator
Shift+Right-click on a taskbar button	Show the window menu for the program
Shift+Right-click on a grouped taskbar button	Show the window menu for the group
Ctrl+Click on a grouped taskbar button	Cycle through the windows of the group

g.) MAGNIFIER

Magnifier is a useful tool that enlarges part or all of your screen so you can see the words and images better. It comes with a few different settings, so you can use it the way that suits you best. Its work is to zoom in or out in order to create what the user views in different sizes.

Magnifier Keyboard Shortcuts

The table below contains keyboard shortcuts for working with Magnifier.

Shortcut	Action
Windows logo key 🪟+ Plus Sign (+) or Minus Sign (-)	Zoom in or out
Ctrl+Alt+Spacebar	Preview the desktop in full-screen mode
Ctrl+Alt+F	Switch to full-screen mode
Ctrl+Alt+L	Switch to lens mode
Ctrl+Alt+D	Switch to docked mode
Ctrl+Alt+I	Invert colors
Ctrl+Alt+arrow keys	Pan in the direction of the arrow keys
Ctrl+Alt+R	Resize the lens
Windows logo key 🪟+ Esc	Exit Magnifier

h.) REMOTE DESKTOP

Remote Desktop Services (RDS), known as Terminal Services in Windows Server 2008 and earlier, is one of the components of Microsoft Windows that allows a user to take control of a **remote** computer or virtual machine over a network **connection.**

With *Remote Desktop Connection*, you can sit at a PC and connect to another PC in a different location (the *remote* PC). For example, you can sit at home PC and connect to your work PC, and use all of your apps, files, and network resources as if you were sitting right in front of your work PC.

Remote Desktop Connection keyboard shortcuts

The following table contains keyboard shortcuts for working with Remote Desktop Connection.

Shortcut	Action
Alt+Page Up	Move between programs from left to right.
Alt+Page Down	Move between programs from right to left.
Alt+Insert	Cycle through programs in the order that they were started in.
Alt+Home	Display the Start menu.
Ctrl+Alt+Break	Switch between a window and full screen.

Ctrl+Alt+End	Display the Windows Security dialog box.
Alt+Delete	Display the system menu.
Ctrl+Alt+Minus Sign (-) on the numeric keypad	Place a copy of the active window, within the client, on the Terminal server clipboard (provides the same functionality as pressing Alt+PrtScn on a local computer).
Ctrl+Alt+Plus Sign (+) on the numeric keypad	Place a copy of the entire client window area on the Terminal server clipboard (provides the same functionality as pressing PrtScn on a local computer).
Ctrl+Alt+Right Arrow	"Tab" out of the Remote Desktop controls to a control in the host program (for example, a button or a text box). Useful when the Remote Desktop controls are embedded in another (host) program.
Ctrl+Alt+Left Arrow	"Tab" out of the Remote Desktop controls to a control in the host program (for example, a button or a text box). Useful when the Remote Desktop controls are embedded in another (host) program.

Note

- Ctrl+Alt+Break and Ctrl+Alt+End are available in all Remote Desktop sessions, even when you've set up the remote computer to recognize Windows keyboard shortcuts.

i.) MICROSOFT PAINT

Microsoft Paint or '*MS Paint*' is a basic graphics/painting utility that is included in all the *Microsoft* Windows versions. *MS Paint* can be used to draw, colour and edit pictures, including imported pictures from a digital camera for example. *MS Paint* is found in the Windows Start menu within the Accessories Folder.

Paint keyboard shortcuts

The table below contains keyboard shortcuts for working with Paint.

Shortcut	Action
Ctrl+N	Create a new picture
Ctrl+O	Open an existing picture
Ctrl+S	Save changes to a picture
F12	Save the picture as a new file
Ctrl+P	Print a picture
Alt+F4	Close a picture and its Paint window
Ctrl+Z	Undo a change
Ctrl+Y	Redo a change
Ctrl+A	Select the entire picture
Ctrl+X	Cut a selection
Ctrl+C	Copy a selection to the Clipboard
Ctrl+V	Paste a selection from the Clipboard
Right Arrow	Move the selection or active shape right by one pixel

Left Arrow	Move the selection or active shape left by one pixel
Down Arrow	Move the selection or active shape down by one pixel
Up Arrow	Move the selection or active shape up by one pixel
Esc	Cancel a selection
Delete	Delete a selection
Ctrl+B	Bold selected text
Ctrl++	Increase the width of a brush, line, or shape outline by one pixel
Ctrl+-	Decrease the width of a brush, line, or shape outline by one pixel
Ctrl+I	Italicize selected text
Ctrl+U	Underline selected text
Ctrl+E	Open the Properties dialog box
Ctrl+W	Open the Resize and Skew dialog box
Ctrl+Page Up	Zoom in
Ctrl+Page Down	Zoom out
F11	View a picture in full-screen mode
Ctrl+R	Show or hide the ruler
Ctrl+G	Show or hide gridlines
F10 or Alt	Display keytips
Shift+F10	Show the current shortcut menu
F1	Open Paint Help

j.) MICROSOFT WORDPAD

WordPad is a basic word processor that is included with almost all versions of **Microsoft** Windows from Windows 95 onwards. It is more advanced than Notepad but simpler than **Microsoft** Word.

It is a text-editing program you can use to create and edit documents.

WordPad keyboard shortcuts

This table contains keyboard shortcuts for working with WordPad.

Shortcut	Action
Ctrl+N	Create a new document
Ctrl+O	Open an existing document
Ctrl+S	Save changes to a document
F12	Save the document as a new file
Ctrl+P	Print a document
Alt+F4	Close WordPad
Ctrl+Z	Undo a change
Ctrl+Y	Redo a change
Ctrl+A	Select the entire document
Ctrl+X	Cut a selection
Ctrl+C	Copy a selection to the Clipboard
Ctrl+V	Paste a selection from the Clipboard
Ctrl+B	Make selected text bold
Ctrl+I	Italicize selected text
Ctrl+U	Underline selected text
Ctrl+=	Make selected text subscript
Ctrl+Shift+=	Make selected text superscript

Ctrl+L	Align text left
Ctrl+E	Align text center
Ctrl+R	Align text right
Ctrl+J	Justify text
Ctrl+1	Set single line spacing
Ctrl+2	Set double line spacing
Ctrl+5	Set line spacing to 1.5
Ctrl+Shift+>	Increase the font size
Ctrl+Shift+<	Decrease the font size
Ctrl+Shift+A	Change characters to all capitals
Ctrl+Shift+L	Change the bullet style
Ctrl+D	Insert a Microsoft Paint drawing
Ctrl+F	Find text in a document
F3	Find the next instance of the text in the Find dialog box
Ctrl+H	Replace text in a document
Ctrl+Left Arrow	Move the cursor one word to the left
Ctrl+Right Arrow	Move the cursor one word to the right
Ctrl+Up Arrow	Move the cursor to the line above
Ctrl+Down Arrow	Move the cursor to the line below
Ctrl+Home	Move to the beginning of the document
Ctrl+End	Move to the end of the document
Ctrl+Page Up	Move up one page
Ctrl+Page Down	Move down one page
Ctrl+Delete	Delete the next word
F10	Display keytips
Shift+F10	Show the current shortcut menu

F1	Open WordPad Help

k.) CALCULATOR

A component of *Microsoft* Windows used for Math work accounting and other related stuffs.

Calculator keyboard shortcuts

The table below contains keyboard shortcuts for working with Calculator.

Shortcut	Action
Alt+1	Switch to Standard mode
Alt+2	Switch to Scientific mode
Alt+3	Switch to Programmer mode
Alt+4	Switch to Statistics mode
Ctrl+E	Open date calculations
Ctrl+H	Turn calculation history on or off
Ctrl+U	Open unit conversion
Alt+C	Calculate or solve date calculations and worksheets
F1	Open Calculator Help
Ctrl+Q	Press the M- button
Ctrl+P	Press the M+ button
Ctrl+M	Press the MS button
Ctrl+R	Press the MR button
Ctrl+L	Press the MC button
%	Press the % button
F9	Press the +/– button
/	Press the / button
*	Press the * button

+	Press the + button
-	Press the – button
R	Press the 1/× button
@	Press the square root button
0-9	Press the number buttons (0-9)
=	Press the = button
.	Press the . (decimal point) button
Backspace	Press the backspace button
Esc	Press the C button
Del	Press the CE button
Ctrl+Shift+D	Clear the calculation history
F2	Edit the calculation history
Up Arrow key	Navigate up in the calculation history
Down Arrow key	Navigate down in the calculation history
Esc	Cancel editing the calculation history
Enter	Recalculate the calculation history after editing
F3	Select Degrees in Scientific mode
F4	Select Radians in Scientific mode
F5	Select Grads in Scientific mode
I	Press the Inv button in Scientific mode
D	Press the Mod button in Scientific mode
Ctrl+S	Press the sinh button in Scientific mode
Ctrl+O	Press the cosh button in Scientific mode

Ctrl+T	Press the tanh button in Scientific mode
(	Press the (button in Scientific mode
)	Press the) button in Scientific mode
N	Press the ln button in Scientific mode
;	Press the Int button in Scientific mode
S	Press the sin button in Scientific mode
O	Press the cos button in Scientific mode
T	Press the tan button in Scientific mode
M	Press the dms button in Scientific mode
P	Press the pi button in Scientific mode
V	Press the F-E button in Scientific mode
X	Press the Exp button in Scientific mode
Q	Press the x^2 button in Scientific mode
Y	Press the x^y button in Scientific mode
#	Press the x^3 button in Scientific mode
L	Press the log button in Scientific mode
!	Press the n! button in Scientific mode

Ctrl+Y	Press the y√x button in Scientific mode
Ctrl+B	Press the 3√x button in Scientific mode
Ctrl+G	Press the 10x button in Scientific mode
F5	Select Hex in Programmer mode
F6	Select Dec in Programmer mode
F7	Select Oct in Programmer mode
F8	Select Bin in Programmer mode
F12	Select Qword in Programmer mode
F2	Select Dword in Programmer mode
F3	Select Word in Programmer mode
F4	Select Byte in Programmer mode
K	Press the RoR button in Programmer mode
J	Press the RoL button in Programmer mode
<	Press the Lsh button in Programmer mode
>	Press the Rsh button in Programmer mode
%	Press the Mod button in Programmer mode
(	Press the (button in Programmer mode
)	Press the) button in Programmer mode
|	Press the Or button in Programmer mode

^	Press the X or button in Programmer mode
~	Press the Not button in Programmer mode
&	Press the And button in Programmer mode
A-F	Press the A-F buttons in Programmer mode
Spacebar	Toggles the bit value in Programmer mode
A	Press the Average button in Statistics mode
Ctrl+A	Press the Average Sq button in Statistics mode
S	Press the Sum button in Statistics mode
Ctrl+S	Press the Sum Sq button in Statistics mode
T	Press the S.D. button in Statistics mode
Ctrl+T	Press the Inv S.D. button in Statistics mode
D	Press the CAD button in Statistics mode

l.) WINDOWS JOURNAL

Learn how to use *Windows Journal* to take notes in your own writing and customize your notes by changing ink color and thickness.

Windows Journal is a notetaking application, created by Microsoft and included in Windows XP Tablet PC Edition as well as the Home Premium or superior.

Windows Journal keyboard shortcuts
The table below contains keyboard shortcuts for working with Windows Journal.

Shortcut	Action
Ctrl+N	Start a new note
Ctrl+O	Open a recently used note
Ctrl+S	Save changes to a note
Ctrl+Shift+V	Move a note to a specific folder
Ctrl+P	Print a note
Alt+F4	Close a note and its Journal window
Ctrl+Z	Undo a change
Ctrl+Y	Redo a change
Ctrl+A	Select all items on a page
Ctrl+X	Cut a selection
Ctrl+C	Copy a selection to the Clipboard
Ctrl+V	Paste a selection from the Clipboard
Esc	Cancel a selection
Delete	Delete a selection
Ctrl+F	Start a basic find
Ctrl+G	Go to a page

F5	Refresh find Actions
F5	Refresh the note list
F6	Toggle between a note list and a note
Ctrl+Shift+C	Display a shortcut menu for column headings in a note list
F11	View a note in full-screen mode
F1	Open Journal Help

m.) WINDOWS HELP VIEWER

This is the page provided by Microsoft to its customers to see when they need help. It has two options: **Offline** and **Online** and is usually represented by a question mark (?). Its shortcut is **F1**.

Windows Help viewer keyboard shortcuts
The following table contains keyboard shortcuts for working with the Help viewer.

Shortcut	Action
Alt+C	Display the Table of Contents
Alt+N	Display the Connection Settings menu
F10	Display the Options menu
Alt+Left Arrow	Move back to the previously viewed topic
Alt+Right Arrow	Move forward to the next (previously viewed) topic
Alt+A	Display the customer support page
Alt+Home	Display the Help and Support home page
Home	Move to the beginning of a topic
End	Move to the end of a topic
Ctrl+F	Search the current topic
Ctrl+P	Print a topic
F3	Move the cursor to the search box

JUST BEFORE YOU PUT ME DOWN, NOTE THIS.

i.   It is important to note that when using shortcuts to achieve any Action, you should make sure that your target area is active, if not, you may get the wrong result. Example, if you want to **highlight all text**, you must make sure that the **text field** is active and if **object**, make sure the **object area** is active. The active area is always known by the location where your cursor blinks.

ii.   The plus (+) signs that come in the middle of the shortcut keys simply means the keys are meant to be combined or held down together not to be added as one of the shortcut keys and in a case where plus sign is needed; it is duplicated or typed twice (++).

iii.   For keyboard shortcuts in which you press one key immediately followed by another key, the keys are separated by a comma (,).

iv.   Most programs also provide accelerator keys that can make it easier to work with menus and other commands. Check the menus of programs for accelerator keys. If a letter is underlined in a menu, that usually means that pressing the Alt key in combination with the underlined key will have the same effect as clicking that menu item.

v.   Pressing the Alt key in some programs, such as Paint and WordPad, shows commands that are labeled with additional keys that you can press to use them.

CUSTOMER'S PAGE

This page is for e-customers who enjoyed this book.

Dearly beloved customer, please leave a review behind if you enjoyed this book or found it helpful. It will be highly appreciated, thank you.

Download Our Free EBooks Today.

In order to appreciate our customers, we have made some of our titles available at 0.00. Totally free. Feel free to get a copy of the free titles.

(A) For Keyboard Shortcuts In Windows

Go to Amazon: Windows 7 Keyboard shortcuts

Go to Other Digital Stores: Windows 7 Keyboard Shortcuts

(B) For Keyboard Shortcuts In Office 2016 for Windows.

Go to Amazon: Word 2016 Keyboard Shortcuts For windows

Go to Other Digital Stores: Word 2016 Keyboard Shortcuts For Windows

(C) For Keyboard Shortcuts In Office 2016 for Mac.

Go to Amazon: OneNote 2016 Keyboard Shortcuts For Macintosh

Go to Other Digital Stores: OneNote 2016 Keyboard Shortcuts For Macintosh

Note: Feel free to download them from your favorite store today. Thank you!

Other Books By This Publisher.

S/N	Title	Series
Series A: Limits Breaking Quotes.		
1	Discover Your Key Christian Quotes	Limits Breaking Quotes
Series B: Shortcut Matters.		
1	Windows 7 Shortcuts	Shortcut Matters
2	Windows 7 Shortcuts & Tips	Shortcut Matters
3	Windows 8.1 Shortcuts	Shortcut Matters
4	Windows 10 Shortcut Keys	Shortcut Matters
5	Microsoft Office 2007 Keyboard Shortcuts For Windows.	Shortcut Matters
6	Microsoft Office 2010 Shortcuts For Windows.	Shortcut Matters
7	Microsoft Office 2013 Shortcuts For Windows.	Shortcut Matters

Series C: Teach Yourself.

Series D: For Painless Publishing

www.ingramcontent.com/pod-product-compliance
Lightning Source LLC
Chambersburg PA
CBHW070925180526
45168CB00005B/2156